Strange
Things
People Say
to
a
L
i
b
r
a
r
i
a
n
.

Captain Flashheart

flashheart.co.uk

Copyright © 2015 Captain Flashheart

All rights reserved.

ISBN-13:978-1502714411

For Alfie

"If man could be crossed with a cat, it would improve man but deteriorate the cat."

— Mark Twain

Contents

Acknowledgements

Introduction

♦Tales from Ventnor Community Library ♦

♦Mutterings from Brighton Reference Library ♦

♦Exclamations & Joy from Ventnor School ♦

Acknowledgements

Thanks to Alfie the cat, Rebekah Guy, Gemma Reid, Mike Banstead, Oliver Gay, Felicity Spunknel, Janneke (for reading it too many times) and all the other contributors and students and patrons who have inspired this book.

Introduction

The world of the professional Librarian is a dangerous and seedy underground of bubbling passions, sexual slavery and unshackled debauchery. Well, maybe it's only the Libraries I've been in.

Anyway, wherever there's a Library, that free revolving door between two opposite worlds, you'll find a stage set for wonders, and that's what this book is all about.

I hope you enjoy reading it as much as I have compiling it.

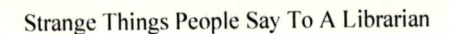

"Have you got Tequila Mockingbird miss?"

Strange Things People Say to a Librarian.

◆Tales from Ventnor Community Library◆

Ventnor Community Library is situated in a small but beautiful georgian terrace at the top of the hill, in the heart of the town of Ventnor on the Isle of Wight.

It's 9AM: Ventnor Community Library

Patron: "Can you take me to the shops to buy a Roast Ham?"
Librarian: "No."
Patron: "Well can I use your kitchen back there to cook it?
Librarian: "Nope."
(disappointment)

Patron: "Do you have the big book with the red cover?"
Librarian: "...?"
Patron: "You know. There's a murder in it?"

Patron (older gentlemen): "I need these in colour."
Librarian: "These are black and white photographs sir"
Patron: "Yes, I need them in colour."

Dad: "Oh fiddle sticks I've forgot mums library card. We won't be able to check anything out today son."
Son (enthusiastically): But dad, I know they take VISA!

And now, for a terrible library joke

Blonde: "Can I have a burger and fries?"
Librarian: "I'm sorry this is a library."
Blonde (in a whisper): "I'm so sorry. Could I have a burger and fries please?"

Patron: "Washing Elephants?"
(Water for Elephants)

✤

*Patron: "Hello, where would you put a book called Twilight?"
Librarian: "Well, we put the books called Twilight over here. Books called Sunset generally go over here, books called Dawn, Dusk and Daybreak go over there, and books called Seduced by The Moonlight go upstairs."

✤

Patron (a rather stern looking lady): "How much does it cost to get your legs waxed?"
Startled Librarian: "I'm sorry, I don't know."
Patron: "Oh for gods sake!"

✤

Patron: "I need a guide!"
Librarian: "For the Alps or the Himalayas?"
Patron (baffled).

Patron: "Sorry to bother you but, is it Beavis and Butthead or Beavis ampersand Butthead?"

A Friday night in the Adult Reading Material Section often unfolds thus:

Patron (alway male, sorry but it is): "Do you have any *Adult* books?"
Librarian: "No sir, it's not that kind of Adult Section."

Patron: "Less Miserables?"

Patron: "Do you have a book on Tom Selleck?"
Librarian: "I'm not sure, let me just…"
Patron (very sincerely): "He's my ex husband."
Librarian: "Really."
Patron: "Yes, he divorced me because I over ate and got fat."
Librarian: "Ah ha."
Patron: "I'm the face of the princess in Shrek."
Librarian: "Okay well here's that book for you."

Patron (clutching a tissue): "Is this a false widow spider?"

♣

Patron: "Sorry, when do you have your swimming lessons? Is it Tuesdays?"
Librarian: "This is a Library?"
Patron: "Yes, I know, but I thought you did swimming lessons?"

♣

Patron (pet birds on his shoulder): "Can I use the internet in here?"

♣

Patron: "Now I don't know the name, but it was on that table at christmas. Any ideas?"

♣

Patron: "The Half Gun?"
(The Afghan)

♣

Patron: "Hello there, do you have 'Lust for Life'?"
Librarian: "Er I used to, but now I'm mostly slightly over tired and in a Caffeine whole."

♣

Patron: "Who wrote Dante's Inferno?"

♣

Patron: "Do you have the Hotmail and Myspace phone numbers?"

And, Or...

Patron: "Can you look up my email address in your catalogue there?"

Plus (occasionally)...

Patron: "Do you have a book with a list of all the websites in it?"

Patron: "Lord of the Files?"

Patron: "I'm looking for a book on blood types, mine has changed recently and I think it's because I've been eating too much raw fish."
Library: "Really I wouldn't have thought so..."
Patron: "Oh yes, it has happened to me more than once now."

🍀

Ring ring:
Librarian: "hello Mike I have someone with me ... Yes a guide book to help her identify the little people that she sees on her lawn ... Yep, yep, okay I'll let her know. I'm sorry we don't seem to have anything."

🍀

Patron: "Hi! I'd really like one of those Interplanetary Loan thingamies..."
(The Interlibrary Loans Service allows patrons to order and access material held at other libraries in the UK and abroad.)

🍀

Patron (holding *something*): "Are these nuts edible?"

Patron: "...a book about free will?..."
Librarian (showing her to the psychology section)
Patron: "But there are no forms in these?"

Patron: "Have you got any of those Agnes Christine mysteries?"

Patron: "Where are the teas?"
Librarian: "We don't serve teas in here."
Patron: "Oh I see."
Librarian: "There's a cafe just around the corner if you'd like?"
Patron: "Well yes, I was hoping to have a cup of tea in here?"
Librarian: "Unfortunately we don't serve tea."
Patron: "Do you have any cakes?"
Librarian: "No."

🍀

Patron: "EXCUSE me. *Why* have you moved the red book?"

🍀

Patron: "Helloo, have you got any books about how to call pigs?"

🍀

Patron: "Now then; is it, *Funny Farm*?"
(Animal Farm)

🍀

Newly met: "Oh you're a Librarian, wow, oh you can suggest a book for me then?"
Librarian: "What are you interested in?"
Newly met: "A little bit of everything i guess."
Librarian (internally): "Ahhhh."

☘

Patron: "Have you got the Wizard of Oz? I just want to read it to the kids tonight before bed."
Librarian: "I don't think we have that at the moment, yes unfortunately it's out on loan, maybe you could watch the movie?"
Patron: "They made that into a movie?!"

☘

The Mysterious Ginger Tabby

"I worked in a Library in Ventnor on the Isle of Wight for a time. Every so often, I would turn around to find a ginger tabby cat half through the doorway or sat on a shelf and I'd have to maneuver him (or her) out. No one ever seemed to know where it came from and the weirdest thing is, there is a black and white photo of a ginger tabby who frequented another Ventnor establishment hung up in the town heritage section. Wooo SpOoKy. Er yes, anyway where were we?..."

※

Patron: "I need a book on taxidermy of small animals, cats, dogs and the like. It can't be large animals! It has to be about small ones."
Librarian: "O-kay…"

Patron (white haired old lady): "...a book on how to make Africans?"
Librarian (slightly shocked): "No, no I really don't think we have."

(Oh, how to make Afghans. Phew!)

Patron: "Do you have a room where I can pump breast milk?"
Librarian: "No."
Patron: "*Oh.*" (disappointment).

Patron: "Do you deliver?"
Librarian: "Er... no." (disappointment).

This happens way more than you would even believe... Patron (young mother with a pram and after several minutes of looking around):

> "What is this place?"

Patron (looking at my name tag, astounded that my last name was "Librarian"): "Well, I guess you had to go into this line of work didn't you!"

Patron: "Can I bring my own books into the library?"
Librarian: "...yes." (I really really wanted to say no).

Patron: "Bonfire of the Vampires?"
(Bonfire of the Vanities)

♦Mutterings from Brighton Reference Library ♦

Brighton University Reference Library

Brighton University is a hotbed of creative talent and really a lovely place to be. The Library is a huge, sprawling building on multiple floors and mezzanines, with space for students to sit, talk and study right at its center.

Patron: "I need a copy of The Gatsby."
Librarian: "You mean The Great Gatsby?"
Patron: "No. Just The Gatsby."
Librarian: "By Fitzgerald?"
Patron: "I dunno."
Librarian: "I think I know what you mean."

🍀

A young, foreign student whom it later transpired had had a rather religious, Mormon upbringing, walked up to the reference desk one morning and said: "What is it all about?"

Librarian: "I'm sorry?"
Patron: "What is life about? I want to know everything."
Well what do you say to that?

Are you paying attention in class?

Patron: "I'm looking for a book about Art Renaissance."
Librarian: "Ah ok, well we have a few books on that period here's one right here..."
Patron: "No I'm looking for a book about *'Art Renaissance'*, the writer?"

Young Student: "I need to find information on a composer, his name's W C something?"

Librarian (really puzzled): "I really can't think, hold on let me ask Michael. Hello Mike, bit stumped, we're looking for a composer 'double you see'"

Mike: "Not Debussy?"

Student: "Do you have any books about people who inspire me?"
Librarian: "Well that's interesting, who does inspire you in life?"
Student: "You pick."

The Indecent Proposals

This happens often and is usually prefaced by a brief period of faux, introductory small talk.

Student: "I'll give you £50 to write my assignment."
Librarian: "No."
10 minutes later
Student : "£100."
Librarian (internally of course): "I'll think about it."

Patron: "The Lion With The Wardrobe?"

Student: "Ma'am, I wonder if you can help me. I'm looking for a book on Injuns."
Librarian: "Right, what kind of Indians?"
Student: "Motorcycle Injuns."

Student: "I'm looking for... Is it 'Angel Dust'?"
Librarian: "No, I don't think it's Angel Dust."

(Angela's Ashes)

Student: "...a book ...about those people who do stuff, you know cool stuff, things that other people can't do..."

(Guinness Book of World Records)

♣

Patron: "Hello I need some help finding a book."
Librarian: "Yes certainly, what was the title?"
Patron: "I'm not exactly sure, but I hid it somewhere last week and now I can't remember where I hid it."

♣

Student: "I need a book on horticulture, do you have any?"
Librarian: "Yes we have lots on that subject, what in particular?"
Student: "I'm interested in learning to grow plants."
Librarian: "Yes okay, well there's books on vegetable plots and also gardening design?"
Student: "I'm trying to grow cannabis."
Librarian: "Right, O-kay."

The Tennis Matches

Patron: "I was watching a film and it had a lady with the surname D something?"
Librarian: "I have no idea? Rebecca De Mornay?"
Patron: "No. Got a young boy in it?"
Librarian: "No idea, Risky Business?"
Patron: "No no. It had a criminal in it, you know like Finnigan."
Librarian: "Ah, what? Oliver Twist?"
Patron: "Nooo I'd remember that. She doesn't marry him, the woman I mean."
Librarian (from some recess): "Great Expectations?!"
Patron: "Yes!"
Librarian: "We have it in the classics section!"
Patron: "No just wanted to know, it's been bugging me all day."

Student: "How long will it take me to read this?"

Phone rings:
Patron: "Hi, um, I checked out a book about an hour ago."
Librarian: "Okay, I remember, is something wrong with the book?"
Patron: "No, the book is alright, but... um... would you like to go out with me?"
Librarian (blushes).

Some libraries now have virtual assistants on their web pages:
Patron (typed): "Are you boy or girl robot?"
Library (typed): "Hello I'm a girl but I'm a human too :D"
Patron (typed): "You type cute"

Phone rings:
Caller (local online newspaper): "We've got a verbal report about a bear attack in Sao Paulo! Are there really bears in Sao Paulo?!"

Phone rings:
Caller: "How much blood is in a typical human body?"
Librarian: "Err, why?!"

Phone rings:
Patron: "Yes, please, I'd like to extend over the phone."
Librarian: "Go right ahead, sir."

Phone rings:
Librarian: "Hello, reference."
Patron: "Is this is the reference department?"

Patron: "Hawthorne Heights?"
(Wuthering Heights)

A colleague of mine mentioned a literary agent he once knew who would often get the phrase by email: "I have done a novel..."
Her response: "Kinky."

Patron: "Oh hi, do you check out books here?"

◆Exclamations & Joy from Ventnor School ◆

St Francis school in Ventnor has just been rebuilt. It's a shiny new look, space age building, for ages 5 - 14 years. The library is small but well stocked and it's right by the canteen for easy spillage reports.

Young student: "Miss! Miss! I need a photo of Jesus."
Librarian: "You mean a drawing? A painting?"
Young student: "No, no it's gotta be a photo miss."

An 8 year old girl approaches the circulation desk and says: "Do you have any books about fairies? But ones about real fairies? How they really live?"
Librarian: "Well let's have a look. There's a story here called..."
Girl: "No! I want to know how fairies really live! Not how people think they live!"
How do you get out of that one?

The 'I know this is a weird question buts...'

Assistant teacher approaches: "I know this is a weird question but... do you have a spare plastic spoon?"
Librarian: "Yes, actually."

Patron: "I know this is a weird question but, do you have any fabric to make curtains?"

Young patron (returning Les Miserables and holding it open): "How does it end?"
Turns out no one had ever read to the last 40 MISSING pages! We got her another copy.

Student: "Have you got any Shakespeare in *proper* English?"
Me: "Do you know, we have…"

Small boy: "...a book about steroids?"
Librarian (Puzzled and slightly worried): "343, over there I think, if we have anything."
Small boy (a few minutes later): "I can't find anything there miss."
Librarian (slightly annoyed): "Have you looked under the right number?"
Oh 'Star Wars'. Oops.

A young girl about 10 years old bounces in, bright as a button, clearly having been sent by a teacher:

Young student: "How do you milk bats miss? Any thoughts?

The same girl a day later (we're friends now):
Young student: "What kind of hinges should my dad put on his shed, do you think miss?"

Teacher (new): "Do you have any ice?"
Librarian: "Noo, why *should* we?"
Teacher (new): "Well I just thought you might have some, ya know being a library."

Patron: "The Cat Who Hated the Sun?"
(Curious Incident Of The Dog In The Night Time)

Young student: "Do you have any books where the kid dies miss?"

Young student: "Do you have any books on the Holocaust? Miss, cos I love, love, LOVE the Holocaust!"

Young student: "I went to Mr.Walker's room and he's not in there. Where would he be instead?"
Librarian: "Well let me just consult my crystal ball and I'll tell you."

Young student: "I've got this homework book miss."
Librarian: "Yes?"
Young student: "Well, can't I just read the Amazon reviews?"

What *are* they teaching them?

Young student: "I need an explanation for why god allows bad things to happen miss, for my Theology class."
Librarian: "huh?"

Young student: "...that book by the man with the bald head and the beard and the funny hat."

Any guesses?

(It was Terry Pratchett)

Student: "Have you got Ben Mellon CDs?"
Me: "Um, sorry gonna need a bit more information"

(Barry Manilow)

🍀

I was Reading Diary of a Wombat (wonderful book by the way) with the teaching assistant, to a group of preschoolers and after reading the title asked the children if they knew what a diary was. A hand goes up at the back and one of the little darlings says: "Its when you have really runny poos." I think we all laughed for a good 10 minutes.

🍀

5 yr old at the desk: "The Cow Power book."
(The Hungry Caterpillar)

🍀

Young Student: "Does the Tooth Fairy have her own teeth?"

♣

Young Student (tilting her head): "Do you have a book on how to build Space Furniture?"
Alas, there was nothing, but how creative is that!?

♣

From a colleague across the sea.
Every time I walk into the cafeteria when the preschoolers are in I get "Hi, Miss Librarian!" over and over. And then "Bye Miss Librarian!" as I leave. It's like being a celebrity!

♣

Young Student: "Who did write Anne Frank's diary miss?

Student: "Miss! I need a photo of the underground railroad."

I explained that people rarely posed for photos when escaping slavery (nor did those illegally assisting them).

THE END

Only kidding...

Elderly woman from Hungary (she told me later) walks in, put both hands on the reference desk and says: "Give me your nakedest romances."
I've been smiling at that ever since.

Patron: "The word JUDGEMENT is spelt wrong in all these books!"
Librarian: "O-kay."

A patron returning a book called The Savvy Girl's Guide To Saving. It was two weeks late and incurred and £3 late fee.

🍀

Patron: "Can you provide me with a job reference?"
Librarian: "Noooo."

🍀

Patron: "Memoirs of a Boy-Toy Soldier?"
(Memoirs of a Boy Soldier)

🍀

Patron: "The Great God Spy?"
(The Great Gatsby)

🍀

Patron: "Do you have any photographs of the Spanish Inquisition?"

A male science teacher approaching the desk with a book containing a picture of the male reproductive organ: "Can I have it enlarged?"

THE REAL END

OR IS IT?

Yes it is.

ABOUT THE AUTHOR

Captain Flashheart is a man who needs no introduction. You all know him as the Queen's own adventurer (and some say lover). He has sailed the seven ancient seas as the captain of the HMS Plankton and HMS Amoeba, captured pirates off the coast of Peru and been saved by many a fair maiden.

Unfortunately, he hit a reef somewhere whilst messing about with ship's monkey and is now shipwrecked on an unknown island – 'the island with no name'.

Contact him if you like, he's got a lot of time on his hands,

flashheart.co.uk